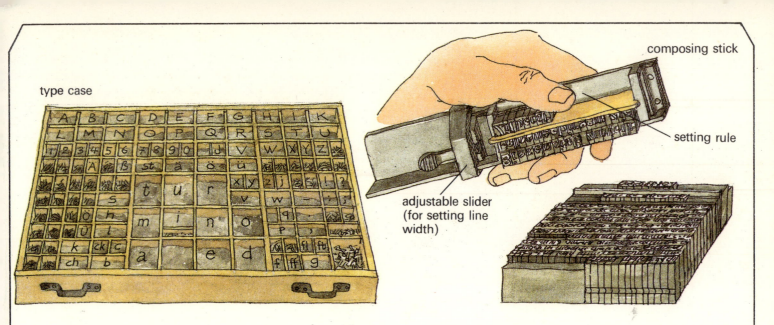

The page of type was locked together so that the lines would not move about. Then it was put on the printing press which you see on page 27. The page of type was covered with a film of thick, black ink. A sheet of paper was placed on top and pressed down with a roller. When the paper was removed it bore the impression of the metal type. The sheets of paper were then hung up to dry.

The bits of type had to be made in reverse, so that when the image was transferred to the paper it appeared the right way round. One of the skills printers had to learn was reading letters in reverse. If you wish to know how difficult this is, try reading this page by holding it up to a mirror!

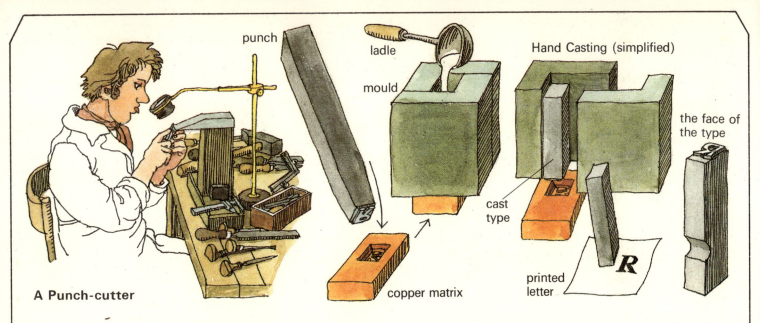

A Punch-cutter

Until the fifteenth century, books were either handwritten or printed from carved blocks of wood, page by page. In the fifteenth century came the invention of movable type – individual letters of metal which could be arranged in any order, and used again and again.

First the characters (letters, numbers, etc) had to be cast. Molten metal was poured into a mould in the shape of the letter. It became solid almost instantly and had to be removed from the mould while still hot so that another type could be cast. This work was done by typefounders. The printer then arranged the bits of type, line by line, until a whole page had been built up. Page 26 shows this work in progress.

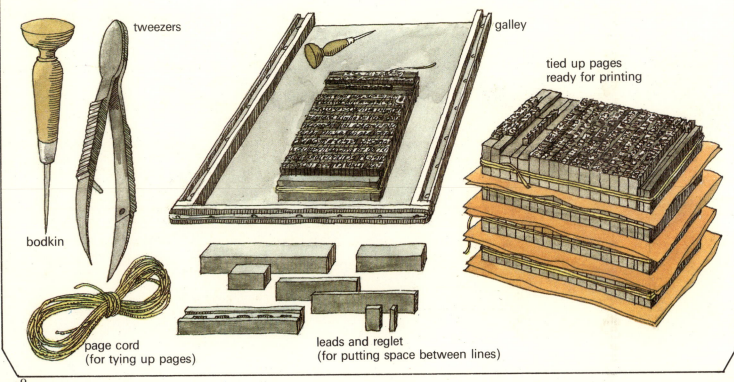

A printing press

Typesetters at work

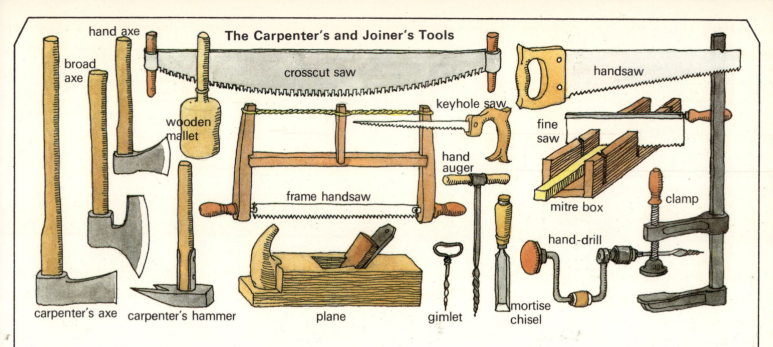

shape. The roof timbers were first constructed in his workshop. After all the timbers had been cut to size, adjusted, and numbered, they were transported to the building site. The numbering allowed the sections to be lowered into place in the correct order.

The other important woodworking craftsman was the joiner. He made such things as chests, cupboards, chairs, doors and windowframes, and the handles for all sorts of tools. He used a vice for holding the wood steady while sawing, a chisel for carving, a drill for making holes, and a plane for making the wood smooth. Page 23 shows joiners at work.

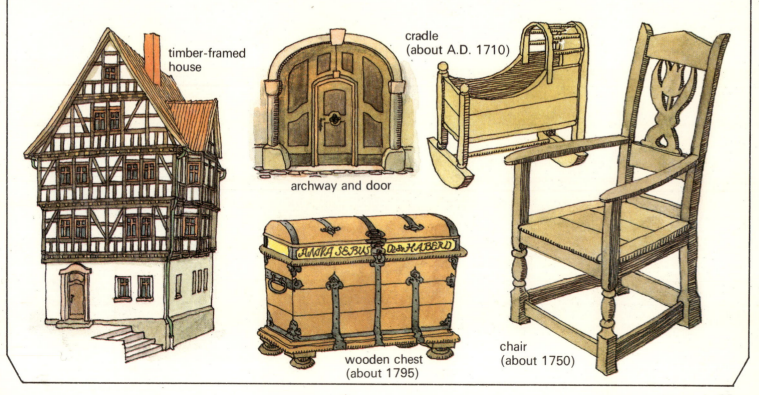

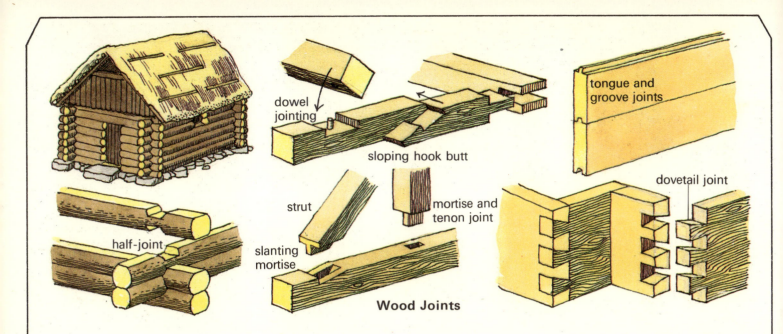

Wood Joints

On page 22 you can see a timber frame house being built. The most important craftsmen here are the carpenters. Some early houses were built of logs with very simple joints to hold them together. Later, however, only the frame was of wood, and the spaces in between were filled in with mud, plaster, and other materials. The wooden structure had to have very strong joints. The two sections of a joint had to fit together perfectly, for otherwise the joint would work loose eventually, and the house might even blow down in the wind! To make his structure strong and rigid, the carpenter used the triangle as the basic

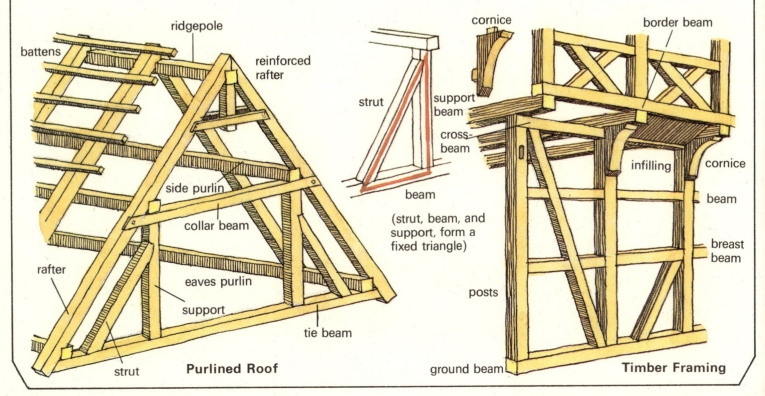

Purlined Roof

Timber Framing

Joiners

Carpenters

Tools made by the Blacksmith

the wheel. As the rim cooled, it contracted and drew tight.

Horses had to walk many miles on rough ground and hard roads. Without iron horseshoes their soft hooves would soon have worn away. When the shoe itself wore thin the blacksmith fitted a new one. This did not hurt the horse because the hoof is dead like the end of your fingernail. The new shoe was made by hammering a red-hot piece of iron into a U-shape. Nail holes were punched in it, and after it cooled it was nailed on to the hoof. On page 19 you can see a wheel being rimmed, and a horse being shod.

The forge

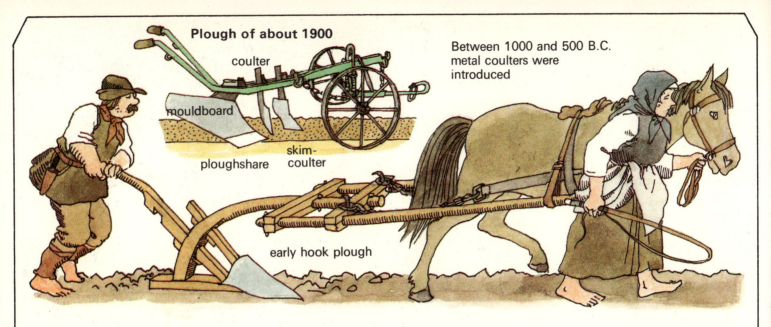

When iron is red hot it can be hammered and bent into a different shape. The blacksmith made iron tools such as hammers, axes, and saws, and parts of machinery such as cogs, and chains. Much of his work was with farm machinery like ploughs, carts used for transport, and shoeing horses. On page 18 you can see the blacksmith's men at work, heating metal over a forge, bending it, and hammering it on an anvil.

Wooden cartwheels were rimmed with iron. When metal is heated it expands slightly. The blacksmith made an iron rim slightly smaller than the wheel. He then heated it until it expanded sufficiently to fit over

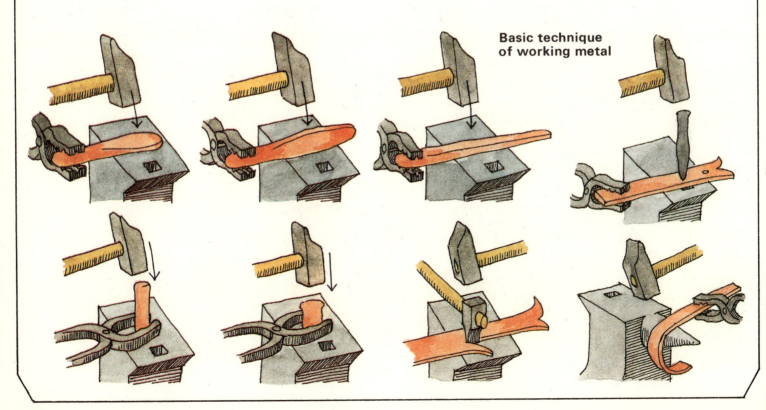

A blacksmith's workshop

A forge

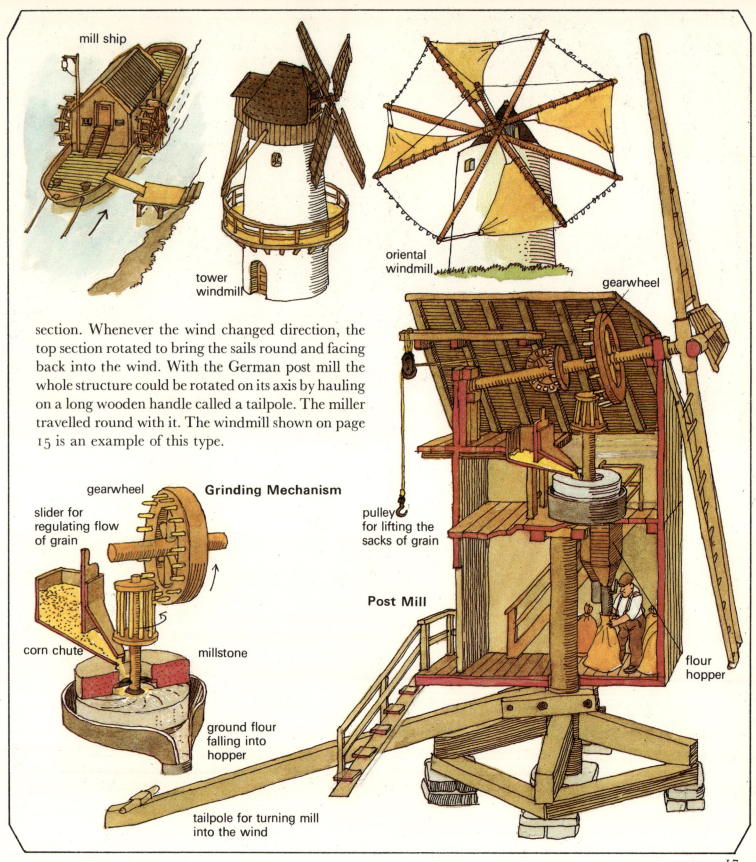

section. Whenever the wind changed direction, the top section rotated to bring the sails round and facing back into the wind. With the German post mill the whole structure could be rotated on its axis by hauling on a long wooden handle called a tailpole. The miller travelled round with it. The windmill shown on page 15 is an example of this type.

A Watermill

Grain is ground to make flour, the basic ingredient in bread. Before mills were invented, grain was ground by hand. It was pounded in a bowl-shaped mortar with a club-shaped pestle. Later, flour was ground between two heavy, circular stones. A wooden pole was attached to the top stone, and used to turn it round on the bottom stone.

Watermills used the power of flowing water to turn the machinery – the water turned a wheel, and the wheel turned the grinding stone. Windmills used the power of the wind. On pages 14 and 15 are a watermill and a windmill. The cross-sections on pages 16 and 17 show how they worked.

The brick-built Dutch windmill had a rotating top

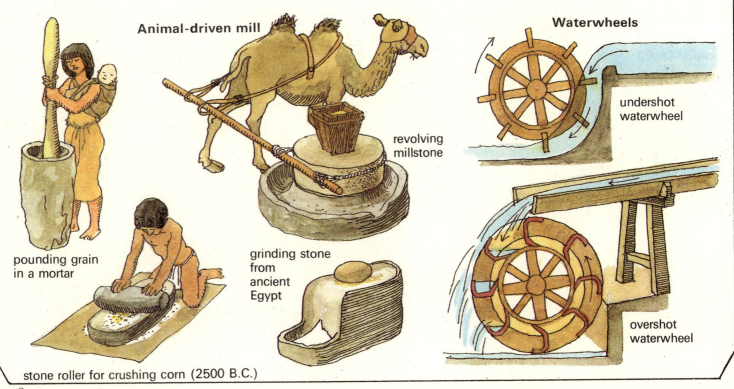

A windmill

A watermill

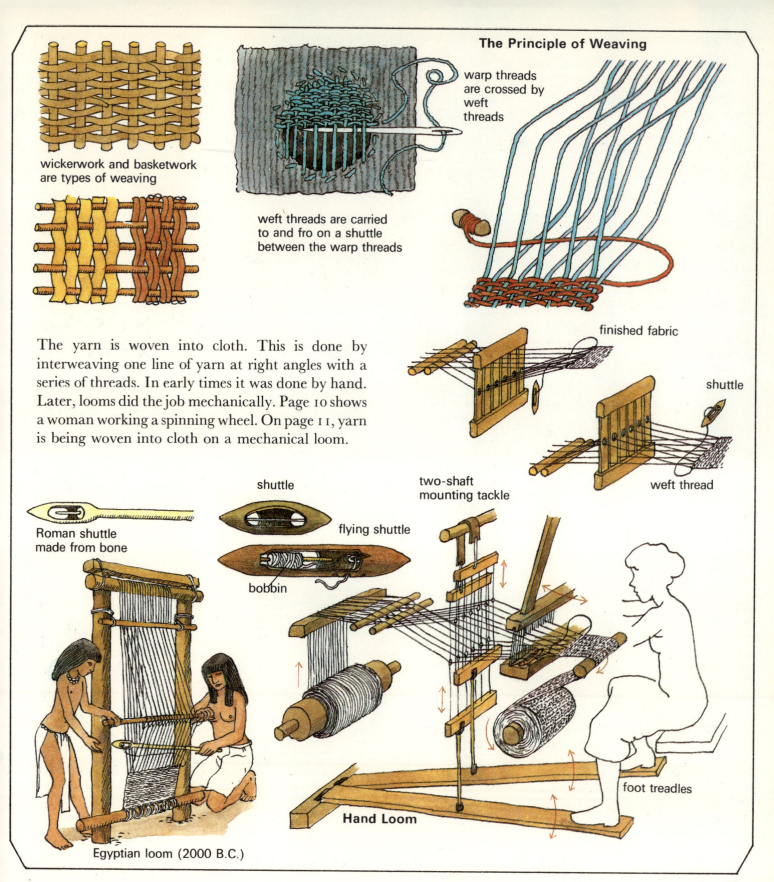

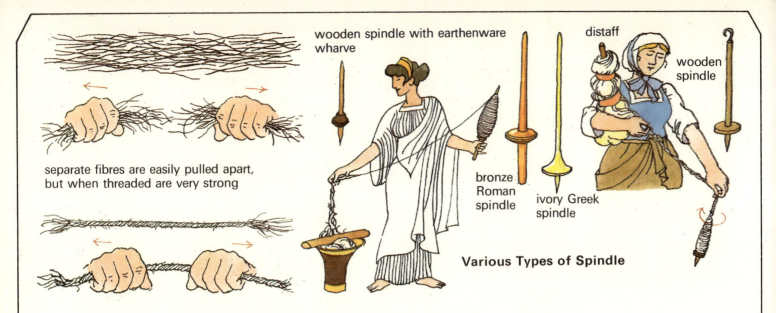

Various Types of Spindle

Words such as 'spinning', 'weaving', 'flax', and 'linen', are some of the oldest in our language. The skill of spinning with distaff and hand-spindle was practised in ancient times. Fibres of wool were pulled off the distaff by hand, twisted between the fingers into thread, and wound on to a spindle held in the other hand. The circular motion of the spindle twisted the threads into yarn.

Later the spinning wheel was invented. The spindle was turned by a cord which looped round the wheel. Early spinning wheels were turned by hand. By the early sixteenth century a foot treadle was used to turn the wheel; this was much better because it left both the spinner's hands free.

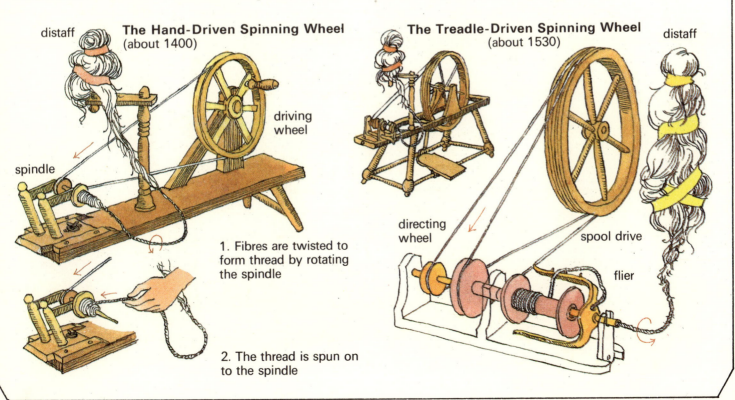

A weaver

A spinner

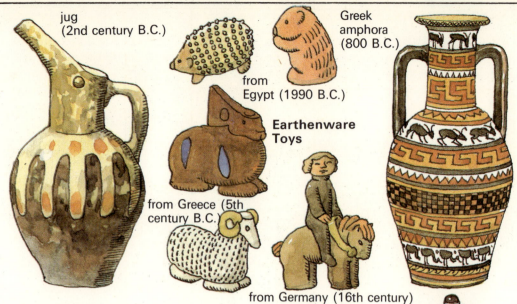

jug (2nd century B.C.)

from Egypt (1990 B.C.)

Greek amphora (800 B.C.)

Earthenware Toys

from Greece (5th century B.C.)

from Germany (16th century)

clay is centred on the wheel

potter presses both thumbs into the lump of clay

to the kiln. The glaze is a fine glass powder which melts in the heat and soaks into the pot, making it waterproof. It can be coloured or transparent, or form part of the pot's decoration.

On page 6 you can see the clay being shaped into a bowl on a foot-driven wheel. A woman is painting on a glaze. Glazed pots are being placed in the kiln ready for firing.

pot is shaped by easing the clay apart

jug, tin-glazed to give white surface

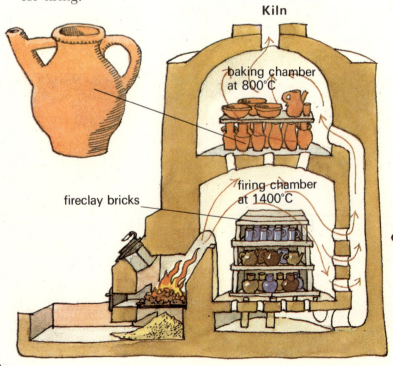

Kiln

baking chamber at 800°C

fireclay bricks

firing chamber at 1400°C

the sides are raised by drawing clay upwards

18th century jug

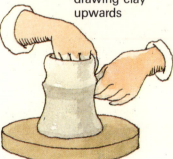

the pot is nearly finished

Pottery is one of the oldest of human skills. The very first 'pots' were made out of wood or stone. The first clay pots were made in Mesopotamia and Egypt around 5000 B.C.

The potter's most important tool is his hand. Although there is a wheel which turns the clay, it is the potter's hand which shapes it into a smooth, rounded pot. On the hand-driven wheel, the potter rotates the turntable with his left hand and moulds the wet, muddy clay with his right hand. The foot-driven wheel leaves both hands free to shape the clay, allowing the potter to work faster.

The pot is hardened in a very hot oven called a kiln, and then left to cool. If it is to be glazed, it is returned

A pottery market

Potters at work

INTRODUCTIONS
Introducing Traditional Crafts

Text by Alfred Könner
Illustrations by Elfriede and Eberhard Binder

Crafts such as pottery, spinning, weaving, carpentry, and forging metal are thousands of years old. Some of these skills developed as early as 5000 B.C. We know this because Egyptian drawings 7,000 years old show these crafts being practised.

Skilled craftsmen were so highly respected that they were glorified in myths and legends. There is an old Anglo-Saxon legend about Wayland the Smith, who you can see opposite. His mother was a goddess, and his father was a king. When an enemy cast him into prison his skill as a craftsman helped him escape – he forged a pair of golden wings and flew home!

In the following pages you can read about the skills and the tools of pottery, spinning and weaving, milling wheat into flour, metal forging, carpentry and joinery, and printing with metal type.

First published in England in 1989 by
Young Library Ltd
45 Norfolk Square
Brighton, East Sussex BN1 2PE

Text © Copyright 1989 Young Library Ltd
Illustrations © Copyright 1986
Altberliner Verlag, Berlin
All rights reserved

ISBN 0 946003 93 9

Printed in the German Democratic Republic

Young Library

Wayland the Smith